I0418540

Dr. Marcia Bailey

She Force

21-Day Devotion and Journal

Edited, Formatted & Published by

Wade Christian Publishing

www.wadepublishers.com

info@wadepublishers.com

She Force

Written by Dr. Marcia Bailey

Paperback ISBN: 979-8-9864810-1-2

E-Book ISBN: 979-8-9864810-2-9

Copyright 2022. All rights reserved.

No part of this book may be reproduced in any form without written permission from the publisher or author.

Acknowledgment

To my husband, thank you for your love, leadership, and support. You are a source of inspiration in my life. Thanks to my children, who unknowingly challenged me to discover my capacity to believe and fight.

Thank you SWATA, and the sisterhood! I appreciate your support! Love y'all, let's do this!

To Karen, thank you for willingly burning the midnight oil and rising while it is still dark with the She Force Devotional!

To Morgan, thank you! You are so talented! You are She Force!!

I give glory and honor to God! It is because of Him that... I can!

Prologue

I believe that as women, we are living in a strategic time on this planet, especially in God's kingdom. We are on the brink of one of the greatest revivals, and the transferring of wealth and influence will make many scratch their heads. This shift is why the devil fights against you so hard and causes chaos. He hopes you get caught up, quit, and become paralyzed with fear.

However, the Spirit of the Lord is about to come through your situation. He will empower you to handle some things that have held you down. God will honor His Word and stretch out His arm to help and deliver. Specifically, some women are thinking about not trying anymore. They have heard a lot of criticism and negativity. God wants to use you this season. You are instrumental to his plan. You are a force to be reckoned with.

Buckle your seatbelt and get ready! God is raising up women that He has called and will use strategically this season, to shift, change, usher, and birth through prayer God's plan and purposes for your family and His people.

My sister, please know:
God has a plan.

He wants to use you to make a difference.
You were born for such a time as this.
You are not alone in your fight.

I want you to know that you are not alone in this fight for your family, purpose, and destiny. You are part of a tribe! You have a village of women, the sisterhood, and we are a force to be reckoned with! You are She Force!

The devil wants you to feel overwhelmed and outnumbered, but you are not alone! You have a SISTERHOOD! We are a group of women that you may never meet and some that you will. These sisters will stand back-to-back and fight the good fight of faith with you. These sisters aren't petty, jealous, or fake! They want you to succeed and win with the hand you have been dealt. We are in every community and work in every arena! We come in different sizes, skin colors, life experiences, and seasons. We must stop allowing the devil to win with his inadequacy, lies, and fear of failure. When we let him win, we forget who we are and the tribe we belong to—giving him the power to set up strongholds in our lives that limit us in our pursuits and keep us from connecting purposefully.

4

The She Force Journal is a 21-day devotion drawn from my life experiences, messages that I have preached, and my time with the Lord.

I will share with you some of the highs and lows of my becoming. There is space after each devotion for you to write down your thoughts and discoveries from your time with God. This space is called, "What is God Saying?"

Journaling is therapeutic and powerful. God has used journaling to help me process life moments, declutter my soul, and to separate His truths and satanic deceptions. It is my prayer that journaling will do the same for you.

Sis, I pray that the She Force Journal will help you to discover and become strengthened in who you are in Christ, and that it empowers you to walk in your authority. I pray that you will find the boldness to be who God called you to be, and take the emotional risk to grow in your sisterhood.

Let's do this, Sisters! Join me daily within the pages of this journal! I want you to decide to open your heart to the Holy Spirit as He illuminates God's Word within your soul and process. Be willing to embrace the awkwardness of the process and do the work! It is your rite of passage as a sister in She Force!

Let's Go!
Marcia Bailey

Table of Contents

Anchored

Psalm 62:6-7 NLT
[6] He alone is my rock and my salvation, my fortress where I will not be shaken. [7] My victory and honor come from God alone. He is my refuge, a rock where no enemy can reach me.

An anchor is defined as a symbol of hope and steadfastness.

My heart is full right now as I reflect on the time this scripture was first shared with me by my oldest Godmother. We lived in Portland, Maine, and it felt like someone just pulled the rug from underneath me, and my world shook. We were financially struggling, and I was a new mom, honestly new at everything. Tears were streaming down my face as I talked with her; I was overwhelmed and shaken by my circumstances. She listened, and when I stopped for air, she took the opportunity to share that I needed to be anchored in the Lord. My faith will empower me to stand through every storm satan could ever brew up. I listened with hope, and she prayed for me. That conversation changed my life and set me on a course to become anchored in the Lord.

An anchor keeps a boat from drifting off and being tossed by the waves in a storm. The same is true for us.

God is our strength, and He is help in a time of need. My sister, if you are going through a storm and feel overwhelmed, turn to God and lower the anchor in your soul by pouring your heart out to Him.

Let's pray:
Father, I am overwhelmed, and I feel lost. I know that You love me and that You will not forsake me. Help me to stand and help me to trust you in my season of confusion. Anchor me in Your love and peace. In Jesus' name. Amen!

What is God Saying?

_____

_____

_____

_____

_____

_____

_____

_____

_____

_____

_____

_____

_____

_____

_____

Trust the Process

Jeremiah 29:11 MSG
I know what I'm doing. I have it all planned out— plans to take care of you, not abandon you, plans to give you the future you hope for.

Process is defined as a series of actions or steps taken to achieve a particular end.

I wish I could say that walking with the Lord and going through His process has been a walk in the park. On the contrary, my journey with God has challenged my reasoning and understanding. I never dreamed of living away from my family in New Jersey. However, that was God's plan for our lives, and it took a series of action steps that led us to become settled in South Carolina.

How did we get from Jersey to South Carolina? By saying "yes" to what we heard and trusting Him to make a way for us. We had to shut down our natural reasoning and trust that God knew what He was doing with our lives. When we decided to leave Oklahoma, we had to say our goodbyes, pack, and move to another state on a Word from God to go and trust that He would take care of us. We had no idea we would pioneer a ministry with multiple locations, but God was working out a future we had hoped for and was His plan for us.

My sister, following God's voice for your life will cost you something. You will have to pay the price of a "yes." That price requires a "yes" and payment of "I will trust and follow your voice."

I know it is much easier said than done, but I'm asking you to give God your yes! Then walk out that yes daily by choosing to trust and not lean to your understanding.

Confession:
Father, I know You know what You are doing with my life and that You have it all planned out.

"God, I Trust You"

_____

_____

_____

_____

_____

_____

_____

_____

_____

_____

_____

_____

_____

_____

_____

_____

What is God Saying?

_____

_____

_____

_____

_____

_____

_____

_____

_____

_____

_____

_____

_____

_____

Embracing Purpose

Proverbs 19:21 NLT
[21] You can make many plans, but the LORD's purpose will prevail.

I would love to ask Solomon what led him to write this? What was it that didn't produce the results he expected? Whatever it was, he said, "People don't waste time planning things that are not in God's purpose for your life."

In college, I ran track, and I had a dream that track would be my ticket around the world. Track never opened the door to travel, but my husband did. You see, I had a plan, but God had called me to a purpose that did not include track for me. His plan would consist of running but running for Jesus! Lol!

I wish I could tell you that I did not grieve my track career for years, wondering about the what-ifs and my potential possibilities. I would watch competitions on tv and say that it could have been me...

Longing for something that is not God's will for you can potentially create a dissatisfied soul. Dissatisfaction kept me in a holding pattern because I kept longing for something that wasn't for me.

It took me some years, but I had to come to terms with the fact that God did not have a track career in His purpose for me. Once I did, I realized that He used the track as one of His development tools for me. God will work your process and journey in for His glory and purposes.

Embrace your purpose... your why.

Reflections:

1. Do you know your purpose?

2. Have you embraced your purpose?

3. If not, what is hindering you?

Reflections:

_____

_____

_____

_____

_____

_____

_____

_____

_____

_____

_____

_____

_____

_____

_____

_____

What is God Saying?

_____

_____

_____

_____

_____

_____

_____

_____

_____

_____

_____

_____

_____

_____

The She in Me

Genesis 1:27 NLT
[27] So God created human beings in his own image. In the image of God he created them; male and female he created them.

Doubt and insecurity are blockers; they block the world and you from seeing who you are.

Have you ever been somewhere, and an unknown woman walks into the room, and her presence begs the question, "Who is she?" Her presence enters the room before her. That was me! Especially in my 20's, I watched and observed others with wonder and admiration, while I questioned if I belonged in the room that others filled with their personalities.

My sister, your presence goes before you! God's Spirit has filled you with the very essence of God, and because of that, there is nothing small or insignificant about you! Refuse to see yourself small! Decide from this day forward to enter every room with confidence and know that I belong here.

Reflections:

1. Describe who you are. What makes you...you? List your most noticeable attributes, good qualities, talents, and gifts.

2. What lies have you heard about her potential, ability, or value?

3. Which one of these lies are you still dealing with?

4. How has believing this lie affected your life?

5. What should you do from this day forward to negate that lie?

Reflections:

_____

_____

_____

_____

_____

_____

_____

_____

_____

_____

_____

_____

_____

_____

_____

What is God Saying?

_____

_____

_____

_____

_____

_____

_____

_____

_____

_____

_____

_____

_____

_____

_____

Blessed and Empowered

Genesis 1:28 KJV
[28] And God blessed them, and God said unto them, Be fruitful, and multiply, and replenish the earth, and subdue it: and have dominion over the fish of the sea, and over the fowl of the air, and over every living thing that moveth upon the earth.

You are blessed and empowered to be fruitful. You are to operate in the capacity of increase and be equipped to subdue and dominate in life. Understand that this should be your state of being. Make a decision not to allow your past failures or disappointments to disqualify you from embracing the woman that God created you to be.

At the core of who you are is a blessed and empowered woman! If this is shaky, you will struggle to believe that you have the capacity to dominate in your life.

Reflections:

1. What is blocking you from embracing the fact that God has blessed you to be fruitful and has empowered you for your life?

Reflections:

_____

_____

_____

_____

_____

_____

_____

_____

_____

_____

_____

_____

_____

_____

_____

_____

What is God Saying?

_____

_____

_____

_____

_____

_____

_____

_____

_____

_____

_____

_____

_____

_____

Courage

Joshua 1:9 KJV
[9] Have not I commanded thee? Be strong and of a good courage; be not afraid, neither be thou dismayed: for the Lord thy God is with thee whithersoever thou goest.

Courageous is defined as not being deterred by danger and pain; to be brave, to stand against the odds.

God has called many of us to go where no one in our family has gone before. We are called to do, create, and build something that is very daunting. God is with us, and we must have courage. My friend, we must be determined to move forward with courage, not only walk into purpose but to face our daily challenges.

When we (my family) left Oklahoma on a Word from God to go, it was scary. We had a church home that became our family, and here we go again, not just moving but relocating to a state I knew nothing about with four young children. We had to move forward with courage and believe that all the loose ends would come together. They did, but it required faith in what God showed us and courage to go where God was telling us to go.

Reflections:

1. What are the things that hinder you from living courageously in life?

2. Are these natural barriers? Or are they thoughts and images that appear powerful?

3. How have these intimidators stopped you from being courageous?

4. Take some time and find scripture to build your faith and empower you to stand courageously in purpose.

Reflections:

_____

_____

_____

_____

_____

_____

_____

_____

_____

_____

_____

_____

_____

_____

_____

_____

What is God Saying?

_____

_____

_____

_____

_____

_____

_____

_____

_____

_____

_____

_____

_____

_____

_____

Be Fearless

Isaiah 41:10 KJV
[10] Fear thou not; for I am with thee: be not dismayed; for I am thy God: I will strengthen thee; yea, I will help thee; yea, I will uphold thee with the right hand of my righteousness.

Fearless is defined as the refusal to be controlled by the emotion of fear.

My sister, the enemy, does not want you to become all God has created you to be. He will use all his trickery to intimidate and paralyze us with fear. We must push past this and fight to be fearless by reminding ourselves that we are not alone in this journey. God is with you, and He will help you.

Reflections:

1. What are areas in your life where God requires you to be fearless?

2. How has fear stopped or hindered you?

3. What can you do to break free from the limitations of fear?

4. Write an "I am Fearless" confession.

Reflections:

_____

_____

_____

_____

_____

_____

_____

_____

_____

_____

_____

_____

_____

_____

_____

"I Am Fearless"

_____

_____

_____

_____

_____

_____

_____

_____

_____

_____

_____

What is God Saying?

_____

_____

_____

_____

_____

_____

_____

_____

_____

_____

_____

_____

_____

_____

Unstoppable You

Joshua 1:5-6 KJV
[5] There shall not any man be able to stand before thee all the days of thy life: as I was with Moses, so I will be with thee: I will not fail thee, nor forsake thee. [6] Be strong and of good courage: for unto this people shalt thou divide for an inheritance the land, which I sware unto their fathers to give them.

Unstoppable is defined as impossible to stop or prevent.

When God told Joshua to lead His people into the land He had promised them, God also told Joshua that He would be with him, and he would be unstoppable. That did not mean they would not have opposition or battles. It meant that no matter what he would face, God would be with him and help him every step of the way.

I want you to realize that as you pursue your purpose, the devil may try to block you, but he cannot stop you! Why? Because God is with you! He will help you get back up, put one foot in front of the other, and show up to fight another day!

Don't allow obstacles to change your mind about your pursuit! God has given you His

Word about the matter. Believe Him and pursue it.

Reflections:

1. Take some time and think about areas in your life that you stopped doing or pursuing. What are they?

2. What needs to happen for you to become unstoppable?

3. Write an "I am Unstoppable" confession.

4. Ladies, say your confessions daily, and let's strengthen ourselves to be all that God has called us to be. There is power in the confession of our faith.

A few scriptures that support confession:

Romans 10:10 KJV
[10] For with the heart man believeth unto righteousness; and with the mouth confession is made unto salvation.

Proverbs 18:20-21 KJV
[20] A man's belly shall be satisfied with the fruit of his mouth; and with the increase of his lips shall he be filled. [21] Death and life are in the power of the tongue: and they that love it shall eat the fruit thereof.

Joshua 1:8 KJV
[8] This book of the law shall not depart out of thy mouth; but thou shalt meditate therein day and night, that thou mayest observe to do according to all that is written therein: for then thou shalt make thy way prosperous, and then thou shalt have good success.

Reflections:

_____

_____

_____

_____

_____

_____

_____

_____

_____

_____

_____

_____

_____

_____

_____

"I Am Unstoppable"

_____

_____

_____

_____

_____

_____

_____

_____

_____

_____

_____

_____

_____

_____

What is God Saying?

_____

_____

_____

_____

_____

_____

_____

_____

_____

_____

_____

_____

_____

_____

_____

_____

Holy Ghost Force

Jude 1:20 AMPC
[20] But you, beloved, build yourselves up [founded] on your most holy faith [make progress, rise like an edifice higher and higher], praying in the Holy Spirit;

I can't imagine life without the Holy Spirit working within me. My life as a young mother was crazy in ministry, and now that I am a Nana, it's even crazier. Not to mention the spiritual attacks that come with being a believer and pastoring.

One day in intercessory prayer in Oklahoma, I noticed this couple just praying in tongues. I was filled with the Holy Spirit, but I overlooked the power of praying in the Spirit. They mentored me in the Spirit, and for that, I am grateful. I learned the force and power of my spiritual weapon of praying in the Spirit.

My sister, tap into your spiritual force and release the power of tongues by praying daily in the Spirit.

Make the commitment to praying daily in the Spirit for 15 minutes.

Prayer:
Father, thank you for your Son Jesus, who is my Savior. I now ask for a fresh refilling of your Spirit or (to be filled) with the Holy Ghost with the evidence of speaking in tongues. In Jesus' name. Amen!

What is God Saying?

_____

_____

_____

_____

_____

_____

_____

_____

_____

_____

_____

_____

_____

_____

_____

Pray For Strength

Ephesians 3:16 AMPC
[16] May He grant you out of the rich treasury of His glory to be strengthened and reinforced with mighty power in the inner man by the [Holy] Spirit [Himself indwelling your innermost being and personality].

Paul prayed this prayer for the church because he understood that we need the Holy Ghost's strength to do what God calls us to do.

We will never truly reach destiny and experience the fulfillment of purpose in our marriages and family without the help of the Holy Spirit. The Holy Spirit is our help; He wants to strengthen and empower you for life.

Raising kids away from family as a pastor's wife was overwhelming. All of my kids played competitive sports; they eventually went on to play at the collegiate level. Need I say more???? Sometimes, I didn't know whether I was coming or going! With the help of the Holy Ghost, I could face each moment and day with strength.

If your strength is low and you feel overwhelmed with everything you have on your plate, ask God to help you by strengthening your innermost being by His Spirit.

Call on Him right now!

What is God Saying?

_____

_____

_____

_____

_____

_____

_____

_____

_____

_____

_____

_____

_____

_____

_____

_____

When Disappointment Happens

John 16:33 AMPC
[33] I have told you these things, so that in Me you may have [perfect] peace and confidence. In the world you have tribulation and trials and distress and frustration; but be of good cheer [take courage; be confident, certain, undaunted]! For I have overcome the world. [I have deprived it of power to harm you and have conquered it for you.]

I wish I could promise you that once you come to the Lord and submit your life to His way and Word, all will go well and without complication. Even if God told you to say yes to that opportunity, marriage, or move, things still go bust, and you could be left wondering what you did wrong?

We came to South Carolina on a Word from the Lord. He told us to move our family, start a ministry, and make South Carolina our home. We were so excited to be in the will of God because we had made moves that were not His will for us. When my husband lost his job several months after starting the ministry, I was confused. Why did this happen to us? We gave God our yes!

People wondered if we would leave, but that was not the plan! We stayed and put our faith and trust in God and His Word. It wasn't easy; we were disappointed, but we decided not to allow the disappointment to move us from our purpose and destiny.

Life will happen! But last orders stand, my friend; trust Him in your disappointment.

Prayer:
Father, I am so confused right now! I don't understand why things look like they are falling apart. Please help me stay focused on your Word and walk this out by faith. In Jesus' name. Amen.

Confession:
I trust the process and the plan that God has for my life.

"God, I Trust You"

_____

_____

_____

_____

_____

_____

_____

_____

_____

_____

_____

_____

_____

_____

_____

_____

What is God Saying?

_____

_____

_____

_____

_____

_____

_____

_____

_____

_____

_____

_____

_____

_____

_____

Undaunted

John 16:33 AMPC
[33] I have told you these things, so that in Me you may have perfect peace and confidence. In the world you have tribulation and trials and distress and frustration; but be of good cheer take courage; be confident, certain, undaunted! For I have overcome the world. I have deprived it of power to harm you and have conquered it for you.

Undaunted is defined as not being intimidated or discouraged by difficulty, danger, or disappointment.

I pray that this scripture will help you face whatever is telling you that you will never be good enough, or you simply don't possess the ability to ever do that thing you know the Lord has called you to. It may even taunt you like Goliath did David, despising his inexperience and age. Whatever it may be, I want you to know I know exactly how you feel! I have had my share of internal conversations with myself that left me questioning my abilities to achieve.

I will never forget the first time I had to speak in front of an audience. I was a shy twenty-something-year-old. I was petrified! I was shaking as I stood. I believed the piece of paper I was holding was rattling in my hands.

It was a fiasco, a mess! I will never forget that day as I was standing before the congregation.

When I reflect on the victories and disappointments in my life, I can now say that the doors I saw open could be attributed to an undaunted stance. It wasn't always easy because life can come at you hard. But don't allow life to bully you! You can stare life in the face and say, "I Am Undaunted."

I hope that you have found strength and encouragement within the pages of this devotional as I share with you some of my victories and, yes, my disappointments. I want you to be encouraged and find your capacity to face life's struggles and say I AM UNDAUNTED.

You got this! What is stopping you?

"I Am Undaunted"

_____

_____

_____

_____

_____

_____

_____

_____

_____

_____

_____

_____

_____

_____

_____

What is God Saying?

_____

_____

_____

_____

_____

_____

_____

_____

_____

_____

_____

_____

_____

_____

_____

_____

Push

Philippians 3:14 AMPC
[14] I press on toward the goal to win the [supreme and heavenly] prize to which God in Christ Jesus is calling us upward.

Paul tells us that God has a goal in mind for us, and we will press our way through bitter obstacles to reach it.

I used to think that once God revealed a plan to me, everything would fall into place. Sometimes they would, but it's not uncommon to have to fight, push and press your way to reach your goals.

Distractions are real! So, you may need a plan of action to reach your goals. Distractions are designed to take your eyes off your goals and the big picture. Distractions must be handled, but you can't allow them to demotivate, discourage, or depress you. You have to fight and push through all of those feelings to continue doing what God has called you to do.

There was a time when my children were in their teen years that we had a conflict with one, and they decided to leave. We were all heartbroken, it was during the holidays, and we had service. So y'all know what had to be done, we pushed! We got up short one family member and went to church. The mother in me wanted to stay home and lament, but God's purpose in me challenged me to push. What am I saying? Pushing will challenge you to the core. However, if we are going to achieve what God has called us to, we have to decide to PUSH!

Reflections:

1. What areas are you challenged in that require you to push?

2. Find an accountability partner that will challenge you when your feelings are dominating.

Scripture Meditation:

1 Corinthians 15:58 KJV
[58] Therefore, my beloved brethren, be ye stedfast, unmoveable, always abounding in the work of the Lord, forasmuch as ye know that your labour is not in vain in the Lord.

Reflections:

_____

_____

_____

_____

_____

_____

_____

_____

_____

_____

_____

_____

_____

_____

_____

_____

What is God Saying?

_____

_____

_____

_____

_____

_____

_____

_____

_____

_____

_____

_____

_____

_____

Win at Contentment

Philippians 4:11-13 KJV
[11] Not that I speak in respect of want: for I have learned, in whatsoever state I am, therewith to be content. [12] I know both how to be abased, and I know how to abound: every where and in all things I am instructed both to be full and to be hungry, both to abound and to suffer need. [13] I can do all things through Christ which strengtheneth me.

Contentment is defined as the state of happiness or satisfaction.

Being content isn't as easy for many because of social media. Especially with it being within our reach on our phones. You go to your phone, get a notification, and you know what happens next? You are scrolling and seeing that everyone looks like they live their best lives, and you feel like you are not.

During the early years of mothering, I felt like everyone else I went to school with was doing much more exciting things than I was. At that time, I changed diapers and picked up toys all day long. I started feeling unaccomplished because I was comparing myself to my friends.

I became discontent and dissatisfied with my life. Discontent is a slippery slope, friend. It will have you in a pity party. I had to change my thinking and internal conversation with myself. So, I stopped comparing and started thanking God for the opportunity to be a stay-at-home mom. Also, with the help of the Lord, I began to focus on my path and purpose for my life.

That season of discontent taught me so much about myself and contentment. I learned that seasons come and go, and they seem to go better with gratitude.

Scripture meditation:

Psalm 34:1 KJV
[1] I will bless the Lord at all times: his praise shall continually be in my mouth.

Reflections:

1. What can you be grateful for?

Reflections:

_____

_____

_____

_____

_____

_____

_____

_____

_____

_____

_____

_____

_____

_____

_____

What is God Saying?

_____

_____

_____

_____

_____

_____

_____

_____

_____

_____

_____

_____

_____

_____

_____

So What!

1 Corinthians 4:3 KJV
[3] But with me it is a very small thing that I should be judged of you, or of man's judgment: yea, I judge not mine own self.

Unfortunately, some people will gossip and offer their unsolicited opinion about what you are doing or not doing. Unfortunately, if you are doing anything noteworthy, the chatter will be unavoidable. When it happens, say, "So what!" Yes, that is right, "So what!" Who are they that their opinions should matter? Because in the big scheme of things, their views do not matter!

Paul came to that conclusion! He realized no matter how much good he did for those he ministered to; they still had something negative to say about his life. He realized he could never convince some of his heart or his intentions.

It can hurt when you are the target of gossip from people you serve. My family had to deal with gossip from people we covered, some we didn't know. I had to learn to forgive their ignorance and disloyalty, because holding on to it only hurts me by potentially making me self-conscious and inhibits me from being my authentic self.

I know it's a lot when it happens, but pray for them, forgive them, and keep being you!

Scripture meditation:

1 Corinthians 13:5 AMPC
[5] It is not conceited (arrogant and inflated with pride); it is not rude (unmannerly) and does not act unbecomingly. Love (God's love in us) does not insist on its own rights or its own way, for it is not self-seeking; it is not touchy or fretful or resentful; it takes no account of the evil done to it [it pays no attention to a suffered wrong].

Reflections:

1. Who do you need to forgive?

2. Who will you commit to praying for?

Reflections:

_____

_____

_____

_____

_____

_____

_____

_____

_____

_____

_____

_____

_____

_____

_____

_____

What is God Saying?

_____

_____

_____

_____

_____

_____

_____

_____

_____

_____

_____

_____

_____

_____

_____

_____

Stand Your Ground

Ephesians 6:13-14 KJV
[13] Wherefore take unto you the whole armour of God, that ye may be able to withstand in the evil day, and having done all, to stand. [14] Stand therefore, having your loins girt about with truth, and having on the breastplate of righteousness;

Paul is telling us that in spiritual warfare, we will need to not only fight the devil with spiritual armor, but in our fighting, we have to learn how to stand our ground.

Satan's job and goal is to get us to doubt our calling, purpose, and capacity. He hopes that the pain of frustration is too intense, causing you to give up and walk away. Don't do it! Don't give up on your purpose, family, or dreams. Don't let the pain make you question if you missed God ... Stand, my sister.... Stand!

When you stand, you are making the decision that you will hold on to God's Word in your heart, that you won't implement plan B, and that you are choosing to believe God over what you see.

It's not easy, but I want to encourage you to take God's Word and say aloud what He told you. Say it right now! Tell the devil you believe what God told you and keep saying this when you feel weary. God's Word will strengthen and empower you to stand, but you must tighten the belt of truth by declaring God's Word over your life, purpose, and situation. Sis, that's how we stand!

Scripture meditation:

1 Corinthians 15:57-58 KJV
[57] But thanks be to God, which giveth us the victory through our Lord Jesus Christ. [58] Therefore, my beloved brethren, be ye stedfast, unmoveable, always abounding in the work of the Lord, forasmuch as ye know that your labour is not in vain in the Lord.

Prayer:
Father, walking by faith and pursuing purpose can be very hard sometimes. I sometimes feel like quitting. Holy Spirit, I ask that you strengthen me to stand and empower me to keep the faith. In Jesus' name. Amen.

What is God Saying?

_____

_____

_____

_____

_____

_____

_____

_____

_____

_____

_____

_____

_____

Stay Woke

1 Peter 5:8 KJV
[8] Be sober, be vigilant; because your adversary the devil, as a roaring lion, walketh about, seeking whom he may devour:

Satan hates everything that God has created ----- We Must Stay Woke!

Stay Woke, derived from the phrase "stay awake," is an internet slang term often used to demonstrate the need for social awareness and social justice --- started hearing it in association with the Black Lives Matter movement.

Staying Woke for the believer is having a kingdom awareness of our spiritual authority and who we are in Christ, because of the devil's desire to kill, steal, and destroy.

Women must realize that Satan hates us, and his devices are designed to deeply wound us in our souls and within our families.

When my children were young, the Lord would tell me to stay alert and double up in prayer and the Word. Friend, we stay alert through God's Word and prayer. When we spend time daily with the Lord, our spiritual senses become strengthened and heightened.

Suppose you feel like you are in a stressful time or a season of warfare. Take some extra time to stay woke by getting in God's Word and praying.

Reflections:

1. Put together an action "Stay Woke Plan" today.

2. Set your prayer and study time.

3. Write down any prayer concerns you may have.

Pray this prayer:
Father, thank you for giving me the authority to bind every devil's device! Holy Ghost, help me stay woke and stay on the wall. In Jesus' name. Amen.

Reflections:

_____

_____

_____

_____

_____

_____

_____

_____

_____

_____

_____

_____

_____

_____

_____

_____

What is God Saying?

_____

_____

_____

_____

_____

_____

_____

_____

_____

_____

_____

_____

_____

_____

_____

Fireproof Your Soul

Proverbs 25:28 AMPC
[28] He who has no rule over his own spirit is like a city that is broken down and without walls.

Satan would love for us to allow what we feel to determine how we show up! Because he knows that purpose, destiny, mothering, and loving requires us to be present! If he can get you in your feelings, he knows he can manipulate your soul and cause havoc in the atmosphere of your home; for he is a manipulator. I want to encourage you, don't let him win!

He wants you to sabotage what God has done or is doing by getting you to see your life and relationships through what you are feeling right now. He wants you to stay hurt until you get angry, bitter, and become a spoiler. A spoiler is someone who is unbearable to be around because they suck the air out of the room. They are horrible to be around because they are not any fun.

Have you heard this about someone you know? Has this been said about you? Friend, don't let the devil win! Don't give him access to your life through your emotions. Make the decision today to talk to your Heavenly Father about your feelings! Spend time praying in the Spirit and allow the Holy Ghost to strengthen you and anchor you in the Love of God.

Pray this prayer:
Father, I no longer want to be led by my emotions! I now realize that my emotional instability can give the enemy access to confuse my life. Today I shut the door by running to you to help me. In Jesus' name. Amen!

Scripture Meditation:

Hebrews 12:12-15 KJV
[12] Wherefore lift up the hands which hang down, and the feeble knees; [13] And make straight paths for your feet, lest that which is lame be turned out of the way; but let it rather be healed. [14] Follow peace with all men, and holiness, without which no man shall see the Lord: [15] Looking diligently lest any man fail of the grace of God; lest any root of bitterness springing up trouble you, and thereby many be defiled;

What is God Saying?

_____

_____

_____

_____

_____

_____

_____

_____

_____

_____

_____

_____

_____

_____

_____

_____

Breaking The Glass Ceiling

Numbers 13:27-30 KJV
[27] And they told him, and said, We came unto the land whither thou sentest us, and surely it floweth with milk and honey; and this is the fruit of it. [28] Nevertheless the people be strong that dwell in the land, and the cities are walled, and very great: and moreover we saw the children of Anak there. [29] The Amalekites dwell in the land of the south: and the Hittites, and the Jebusites, and the Amorites, dwell in the mountains: and the Canaanites dwell by the sea, and by the coast of Jordan. [30] And Caleb stilled the people before Moses and said, Let us go up at once, and possess it; for we are well able to overcome it.

God gave the people the opportunity to take a look at the land He wanted them to have. When they went, they saw the land, but the size of the people scared them. They thought they could not take what God had given them. They saw the land, but believed they did not have the strength to break through intimidation to possess.

Does this resonate with you? God shows you an image of what He wants to do in you, through you, for you, and fear sets in because of the resistance.

God is calling us as women to go into places where no woman has gone before, to do some things that women have not done before! But it requires us to have faith and not allow our gender or the opposite sex to intimidate us into thinking we are not strong enough. Sis, you are strong enough because the greater one is living inside of you. You just have to keep pushing. If something has knocked you down, it is time to get back up.

Please don't allow the "no," or how big it is to intimidate you! I want you to write down the vision, and speak the vision! I want you to believe that you are well able to overcome the obstacles and resistance before you.

Pray this prayer:
Father, I thank you for being with me! Thank you for equipping me to break through barriers and ceilings of resistance. You have given me a vision of my life. I have decided to believe only in You and keep going. In Jesus' name. Amen!

Scripture Meditation:

1 John 4:4 KJV
[4] Ye are of God, little children, and have overcome them: because greater is He that is in you, than he that is in the world.

Habakkuk 2:2-3 KJV
[2] And the Lord answered me, and said, Write the vision, and make it plain upon tables, that he may run that readeth it. [3] For the vision is yet for an appointed time, but at the end it shall speak, and not lie: though it tarry, wait for it; because it will surely come, it will not tarry.

Reflections:

1. Write the vision down.

Reflections:

_____

_____

_____

_____

_____

_____

_____

_____

_____

_____

_____

_____

_____

_____

What is God Saying?

_____

_____

_____

_____

_____

_____

_____

_____

_____

_____

_____

_____

_____

_____

_____

_____

Be the "She" You Need

Matthew 22:37-39 KJV
[37] Jesus said unto him, Thou shalt love the Lord thy God with all thy heart, and with all thy soul, and with all thy mind. [38] This is the first and great commandment. [39] And the second is like unto it, Thou shalt **love thy neighbour as thyself.**

As women, we may unknowingly place the need to feel loved by everyone in our lives. We are overlooking that it is also essential for us to love ourselves.

Jesus explained to the lawyer that we are to love God with all of our souls, and secondly, we are to love our neighbors as ourselves. It also implies that you really can't love others if you don't love the person you see in the mirror every day.

God also wants you to embrace the love that He has for you. We put so much weight and value on others loving us, and they should. But if they don't communicate it properly to you, I want you to know that you have a Father in Heaven waiting to love you by telling you how much you mean to Him.

So, let's stop waiting on others to show how much they love you and decide to love yourself daily by showing self-care.

We can start doing this by simply loving on ourselves and doing the following:
- Speak positively about yourself.
- Get adequate rest.
- Do something you enjoy weekly.
- Laugh more.

Jesus also said to love your neighbor as yourself. I have learned as a woman in ministry leadership that sometimes some women are the worst supporters of other women because of jealousy. They don't cheer, support or compliment because they low-key want to be them. Yet, they want what they don't give! I want to encourage you to be the "She" you need! Give generously the support and encouragement you desire. Don't side-eye or dissect with the goal to copy! Thank God for her, and allow her light to inspire you to give God praise.

Sis, God, is waiting to show you love and teach you how to love yourself. He is also waiting on you to celebrate the sister who may be standing right before you center stage. Ladies, let's love our neighbors as ourselves.

Scripture meditation:

Psalm 139:14 AMPC
[14] I will confess and praise You for You are fearful and wonderful and for the awful wonder of my birth! Wonderful are Your works, and that my inner self knows right well.

Reflections:

1. After reading this scripture, what thoughts do you have about yourself?

Pray this prayer:
Father, I desire to encounter your love at a deeper level. I also desire to be a conduit of your love for others. Help me not to allow fear or any insecurity to keep me from loving hard and living in the light of your love. In Jesus' name. Amen!

Reflections:

_____

_____

_____

_____

_____

_____

_____

_____

_____

_____

_____

_____

_____

_____

_____

_____

What is God Saying?

_____

_____

_____

_____

_____

_____

_____

_____

_____

_____

_____

_____

_____

_____

_____

_____

_____

She Force

Exodus 3:22 KJV
[22] But every woman shall borrow of her neighbour, and of her that sojourneth in her house, jewels of silver, and jewels of gold, and raiment: and ye shall put them upon your sons, and upon your daughters; and ye shall spoil the Egyptians.

God told Moses that He had a plan to deliver Israel from slavery! He was going to bring them out, but they were not going to go out broke! He was going to strip the Egyptians of their wealth, and He was going to use women to execute the recompense part of the plan.

During these times, women were very marginalized and subjugated! And, let's not add into the equation, enslaved! However, God understood how He made woman, and He knew that even though she was enslaved and traumatized, she could take her pain and turn it on the enemy.

Sis, that's what I'm telling us to do right now! Take that pain, disappointment, and anger, turn it on the devil, and make him pay for what he has done. God had confidence in women then, and I want us to know He has confidence in us now!

I also want you to realize that you are not alone in the fight and mission. God has a squad of women who will be your sisters in the fight that you can trust to have your back. I know you may have been disappointed in the past, but don't allow that experience to close your heart to sisterhood. It's a new season, and God is doing a new thing in the hearts of women.

God is raising up an army of women to handle some business for the kingdom. Will you join the sisterhood? Will you join She Force?

If you said yes, don't miss this opportunity to be a part of what God is doing now!

- Show up again to gatherings of women.
- Exchange numbers.
- Open your heart to relationships.
- Become concerned about your sisters.
- Be your sister's keeper.

Scripture Meditation:

Ecclesiastes 4:9 KJV
[9] Two are better than one; because they have a good reward for their labour.

Matthew 18:19-20 KJV

[19] Again I say unto you, That if two of you shall agree on earth as touching any thing that they shall ask, it shall be done for them of my Father which is in heaven. [20] For where two or three are gathered together in my name, there am I in the midst of them.

Pray this prayer of commitment:

Father, I open my heart to what you are doing this season. I understand that you are doing a new thing, and I make the decision to step into a place of faith and trust you to lead me. I commit to the sisterhood, and say yes to the call to be a part of your army - She Force. In Jesus' name. Amen!

What is God Saying?

About the Author

Dr. Marcia Bailey is the Co-Founder of Right Direction Church International in Columbia, Orangeburg, Florence, and Fort Mill, SC. She is also the mother of four adult children and a grandmother of six. She has lived in her native state of New Jersey, Maine, and Oklahoma before she and her family relocated to South Carolina in 1995. Working beside her husband, Bishop Herbert Bailey, they have been pastoring a thriving, non-denominational church for 26 years of pastoral ministry.

Dr. Marcia pursued a Bachelor's degree in Special & Elementary Education at Seton Hall University in South Orange, NJ. Over the last twenty-six years, she has worked beside her husband as Assistant Pastor of Sanctuary Evangelistic Church in Tulsa, OK, and in the Church of God in Christ in Portland, ME. Before she and her husband founded RDCI, she was a facilitator of Women's Counseling Groups and a Director of Christian Education. In April 2004, Pastor Marcia was honored with a Doctorate of Divinity degree from St. Thomas Christian College in Jacksonville, FL.

Her passion for God, and her experience and training in education, has uniquely qualified her as an administrator, anointed teacher, and preacher of the Word of God. She has a strong anointing for prayer and intercession and is used by God in the Word of Wisdom and Discerning of Spirits. Dr. Marcia's ministry communicates a message of faith, power, and whole-life prosperity. She considers it an honor to be used by God and do His Kingdom's work.

www.ingramcontent.com/pod-product-compliance
Lightning Source LLC
Chambersburg PA
CBHW060342130626
46553CB00003B/1090